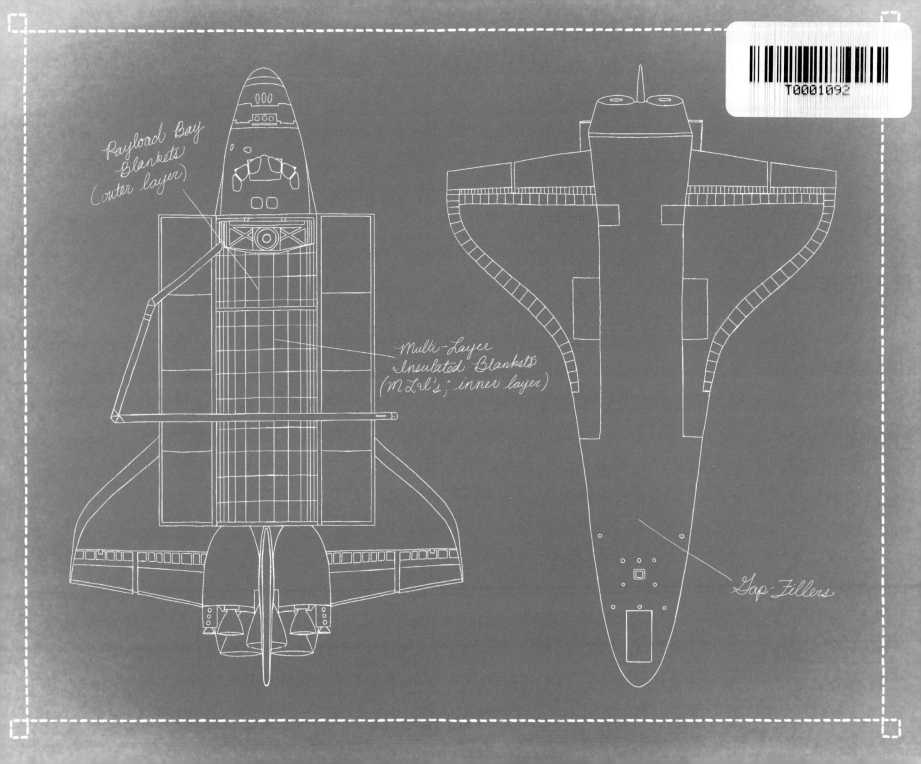

Payload Bay
Blankets
(outer layer)

Multi-Layer
Insulated Blankets
(MLI's; inner layer)

Gap-Fillers

Sew Sister

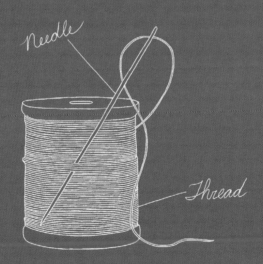

Needle

Thread

To my family, and to
Jean Wright and NASA's
extraordinary seamstresses.
— Elise Matich

To my loving partner Ken Kremer,
whose shared passion for space and
photography brought us together. I still see stars in
your eyes! And to my children—Jennifer, Jessica, and
Edsel. You are my universe.
—Jean Wright

© 2023 by Elise Matich

Hardcover ISBN 978-0-88448-982-5 · Library of Congress Control Number: 2023937761

10 9 8 7 6 5 4 3 2 1

Tilbury House Publishers · www.tilburyhouse.com

Designed by Frame25 Productions
Printed in South Korea

Sew Sister

The Untold Story of
Jean Wright and NASA's
Seamstresses

Written and Illustrated by
Elise Matich

TILBURY HOUSE PUBLISHERS

This is a ship that astronauts sailed
to the edges of air and gravity:
a space shuttle, built to orbit the
Earth, sped by rockets, and
covered with
. . . blankets.

It may sound strange, since few people think
about sewing as high technology,
but each shuttle soared through star-
scattered space in a coat made
of panels of fabric.

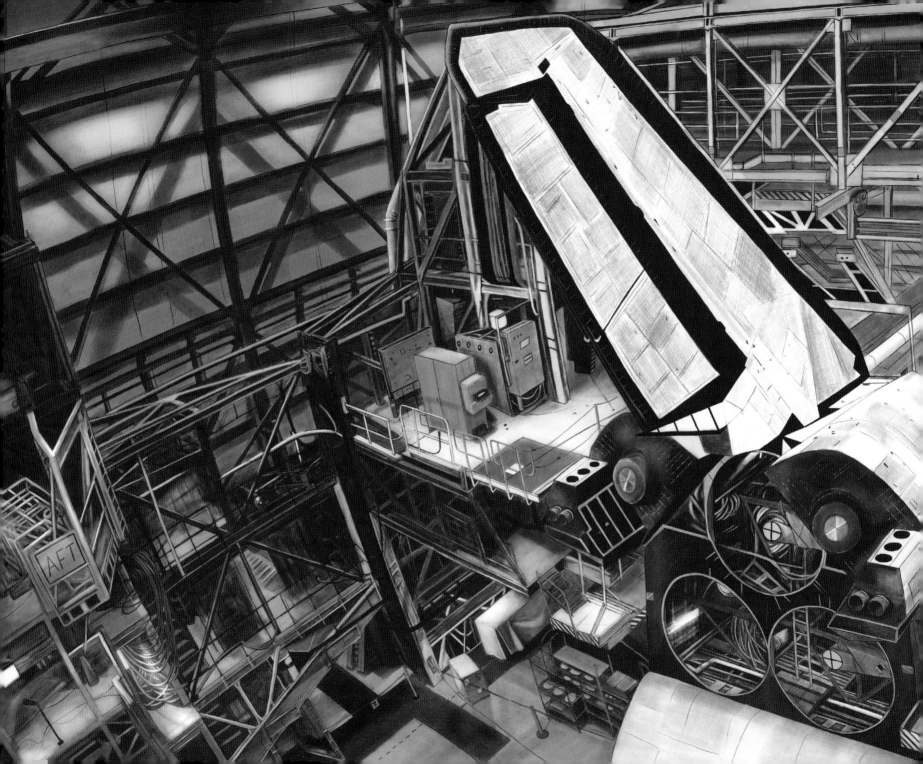

Thousands of hands made the space shuttles fly,
and this is the story of two of them—
a story of thread,
persistence, and dreams,
and of Jean,
who made blankets for NASA.

Jean learned to sew,
with her twin sister, Joan,
in a town known as Flint, in Michigan.
Ms. Hansford, next door, had no kids of her own,
and one morning, she offered to teach them.

She let them make her steam iron hiss,
as she schooled them in simple mysteries,
like how to match bits of plaid in a seam,
and to press it,
just like a real seamstress.

Jean's home was not as happy as some;
it was sewing that soothed the brokenness.
Frays, she could fix,
and tears, she could mend,
and in cloth, she found freedom and comfort.

Soon, she could sew new clothes for her dolls
out of remnants and rag-bin finery.
She learned how to pin,
and gather, and trim,
and to paint quiet pictures with quilting.

Jean was thirteen when, one summer night,
the world wondered at two brave astronauts,
who took silent steps on crater-cracked land
in an untroubled ocean of
moon dust.

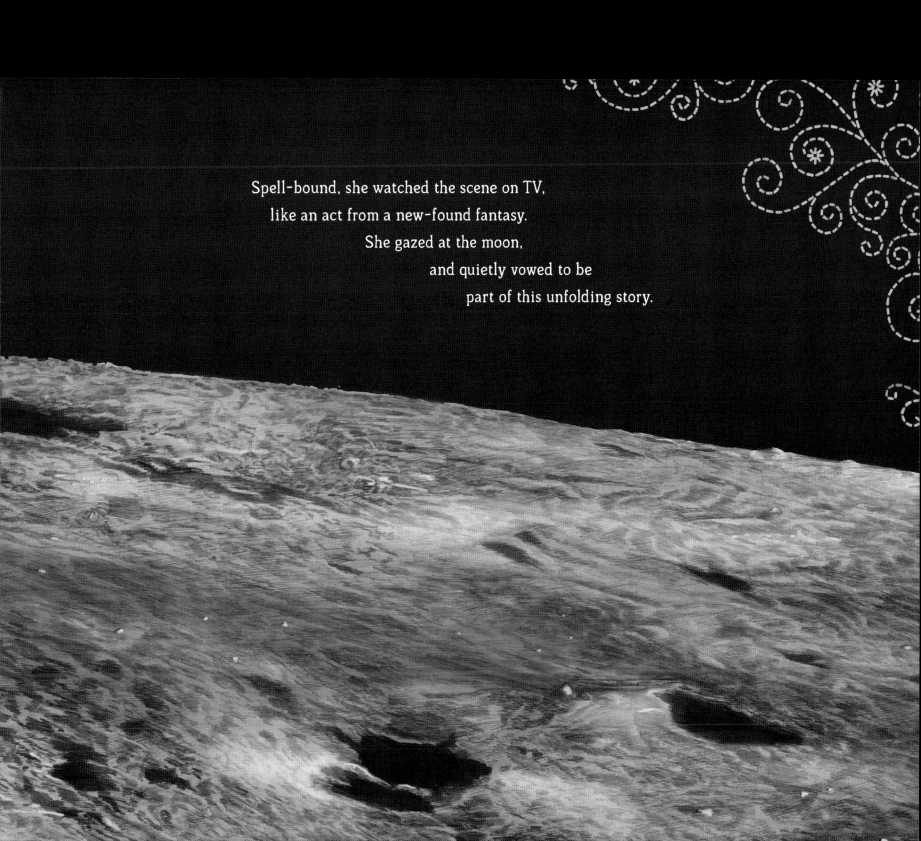

Spell-bound, she watched the scene on TV,
like an act from a new-found fantasy.
She gazed at the moon,
and quietly vowed to be
part of this unfolding story.

But what can I do?
Jean thought as she worked,
saving stories she read in magazines,
on launches and flights and missions and crews;
she filled scrapbooks with hundreds of clippings.

Proudly, she sent new crew-patch designs,
sketched in crayon, to moon-bound astronauts.
And they wrote her back! (to kindly decline),
still, it taught her to try — and be patient.

It was a time when many kids dreamed
of becoming a NASA scientist,
or piloting ships with rockets for sails
to the shores of the moon, or beyond it.

It was an age of challenge and change,
and, for women, new opportunities,
but Flint offered few to girls without means
to afford the expenses of college.

Jean married young. Her husband's career
(in the navy) meant lots of traveling.
At last, he asked Jean
to choose a new home;
she knew just where she wanted to settle.

She moved to a town on Florida's coast,
near a point known as Cape Canaveral,
where rockets took off,
and space shuttles soared.
It was thrilling to simply be near them.

Everything changed one morning, by chance.
In the paper, she saw a photograph
of someone at work on something that looked
like a *quilt*, in a story on NASA.

It was a seamstress, needle in hand.
In amazement, Jean read the article;
it told of a team of women who sewed
special blankets to cover the shuttles.

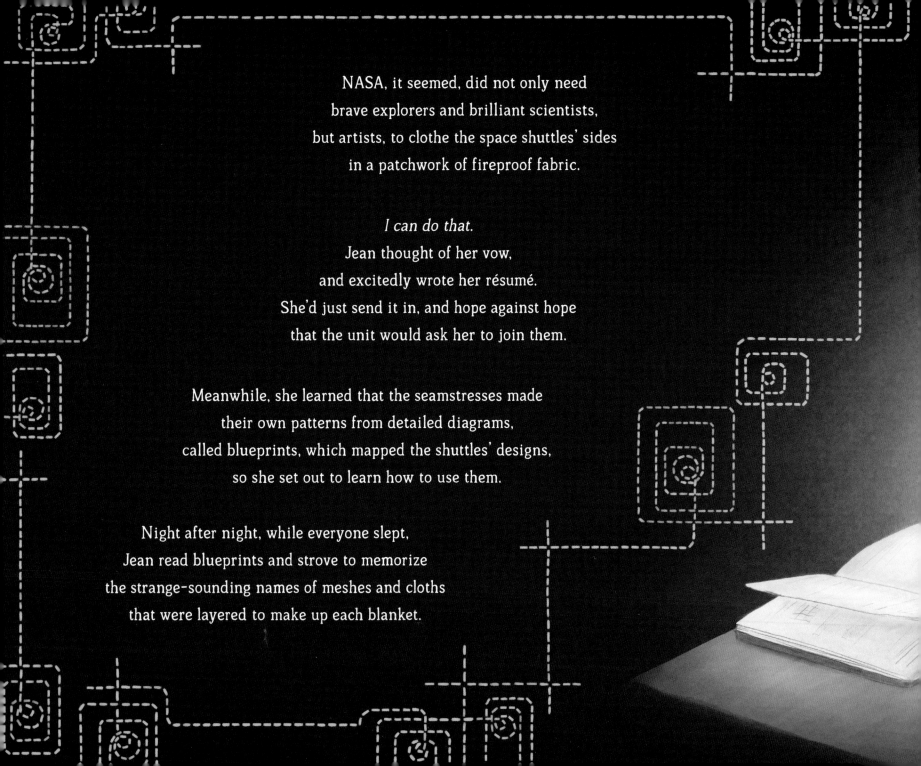

NASA, it seemed, did not only need
brave explorers and brilliant scientists,
but artists, to clothe the space shuttles' sides
in a patchwork of fireproof fabric.

I can do that.
Jean thought of her vow,
and excitedly wrote her résumé.
She'd just send it in, and hope against hope
that the unit would ask her to join them.

Meanwhile, she learned that the seamstresses made
their own patterns from detailed diagrams,
called blueprints, which mapped the shuttles' designs,
so she set out to learn how to use them.

Night after night, while everyone slept,
Jean read blueprints and strove to memorize
the strange-sounding names of meshes and cloths
that were layered to make up each blanket.

Months slowly passed, and Jean tried again;
she revised and resent her résumé.
Then, one afternoon, the telephone rang.
Her heart started to race—
it was NASA.

A seamstress had left the closely-knit team
of technicians known as the Sew Sisters,
who fashioned the quilts
that the space shuttles wore;
their director was asking to meet her!

Jean's skills impressed
the interview team,
and her passion for space persuaded them.
She barely believed the news she received
saying *she* would be working for NASA!

Jean's quiet dream was suddenly real,
and she found she was not the only girl
who'd whispered a pledge
that night, to the moon,
and who'd kept it with thread and a needle.

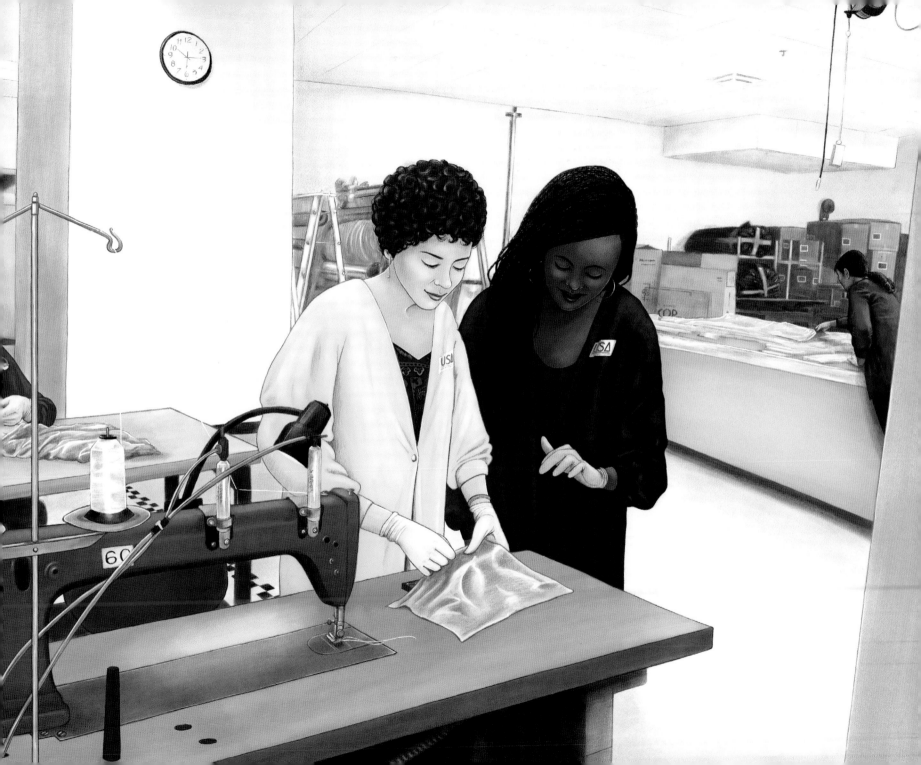

The Sew Sisters' work protected the ships
as they ferried their fearless passengers
from Earth into space,
and space back to Earth;
every quilt had a place and a purpose.

Some could withstand the furious heat
caused by friction,
as ship met atmosphere.
A crystal, called quartz, was used in the cloth;
the lint littered the room with its shimmer.

Hidden beneath these outermost quilts
was another set:
thin and delicate.
Each one was hand-stitched
to keep the crew safe
from the sear of the sun's radiation.

Some of the most unusual quilts
would be sewn by machine—
surprisingly, a sturdy antique from 1914,
built for saddles, but perfect for spacecraft!

Giant, white rings,
these blankets suppressed
the unbearable roaring of engine noise,
and had to be sewn directly to domes
that curve out from the base of each shuttle.

Jean didn't hold a tasseled degree,
and her skill seemed a shy and simple one,
when engineers tossed out jokes as they passed
about mending their jackets or trousers.

Simple—perhaps, and gentle, and old—
but the boldest of dreams depend upon
the simplest things to quietly bring
the most daring of quests into harbor.

Jean loved to watch the shuttles take off.
She would smile to
know her handiwork
would sprint with each ship
through sunrise and clouds
as it chased new adventures above her.

But after one launch,
the worried news came
that *Atlantis* had torn a blanket loose.
Jean thought of the ship—
that dauntless, old friend,
and the heroes in orbit aboard her.

There was a chance that, on their return,
the loose fabric might pull more blankets up,
creating a blaze of blistering heat,
risking damage
—or even disaster.

Back on the ground,
the Sew Sisters raced
to make blankets to test in wind tunnels,
to see if the crew
could keep the small tear
from exposing the
shuttle to danger.

Jean and her team helped engineers try
using needles to sew the blankets down.
Though some, shaped like hooks,
seemed likely to work,
the team's test runs uncovered a problem.

The astronauts' gloves were bulky and stiff,
not intended for nimble needlework.
They fumbled the deft and delicate task
meant for seamstresses' capable fingers.

Thread wouldn't do,
but what else on board
could the astronauts use as a fastener?
Then, someone recalled that the medical kit
was equipped with a surgical stapler.

Rigorous tests
suggested that, yes!
With the staples inserted carefully,
Atlantis and crew could safely return,
so the astronauts put
on their spacesuits.

A camera on board allowed Jean to watch
as an astronaut tucked the blanket back
and stapled it down,
with cumbersome care,
to a part of the ship called the OMS pod.

Thrilled and relieved,
the Sew Sisters cheered
as the shuttle,
with billowed parachute,
touch gracefully down,
its blankets intact,
on a bright afternoon,
one week later.

After their flight,
Atlantis's crew
came to thank
the intrepid seamstresses
who'd helped bring them home
to loved ones and friends
with their labor of scissors and stitches.

Journeys and dreams must come to an end,
and the shuttles now rest from wandering,
as new missions search
the limitless skies
that still beckon us endlessly onward.

Someday, perhaps,
you'll pilot new ships
to strange planets or far-flung galaxies,
or maybe you'll bring the wayfarers home
with the skill in the tips of your fingers.

Stitches are small,
and so was their part
in the shuttles' amazing voyages,
but very small things
can lift mighty wings
on the heels of the highest adventures.

Author's Note

After the shuttle program ended in 2011, Jean Wright continued to support NASA's mission of space exploration as a speaker and consultant and as a docent at the *Atlantis* exhibit at the Kennedy Space Center Visitor Complex. I met her in 2019, while touring the Kennedy Space Center with my family. I was astonished at the amount of sewing involved in building and maintaining the space shuttles and captivated by the untold story of the Sew Sisters. Telling it has reinforced my respect for the extraordinary power of ordinary things. Adventures are known for the icons they produce, like *Atlantis* and the courageous astronauts of the shuttle program. But they are built on the strength of simple materials, like fabric and thread, and on the quiet artisanship of people like Jean. It is fitting that the greatest feats of human exploration should be grounded in humble domestic arts. I hope that Jean's story will help to illuminate the value and possibilities of skilled craftsmanship and inspire admiration for the people who make it their lives' work. Here are a few more glimpses into the hidden history of space-bound stitches and the unsung heroines who made them.

Although space shuttles could be reused (unlike the Apollo capsules), their thermal blankets and barriers needed to be replaced frequently. Over 35 years, 18 NASA seamstresses created thousands of blankets for the shuttles' 135 missions. Officially known as "Aerospace Composite Technicians (Soft-Goods)," the seamstresses called themselves the Sew Sisters. This photo shows the team in 2011. Jean is in the bottom row, third from the left. Not shown is Pilar Valdivieso, whose picture in *Florida Today* inspired Jean to apply for the job. Jean was the last seamstress hired for the program. She started work on Valentine's Day, 2005. (Jean Wright photo)

1,400 flexible insulated blankets (FIBs) cover nearly the entire outside of the space shuttles. Varying from ½ inch to 2 inches thick, they were made from quartz fabric, silica felt batting, and fiberglass backing. FIBs could withstand temperatures of 650 to 1,300 degrees Fahrenheit, generated by friction, as the shuttles reentered Earth's atmosphere. The areas of the shuttles exposed to the highest temperatures were the nose and leading wing edges. These were protected by reinforced carbon-carbon (RCC), also a cloth-based material, which could withstand temperatures of over 3,000 degrees.

The undersides of the space shuttles were covered with silica tiles that could withstand temperatures of 2,300 degrees Fahrenheit. The Sew Sisters hand-stitched fabric "gap-fillers" to seal the spaces between tiles.

FIBs were quilted on a 10-foot-tall, 30-needle sewing machine. It quilted large squares called production units (PUs), from which the seamstresses cut each uniquely shaped blanket.

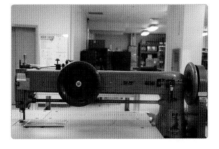

"Lurch" was the nickname given to the 1914 Singer sewing machine used for creating the shuttles' dome heat shield blankets, which encircle each engine. Originally used in saddle-making, the machine was purchased by NASA from a warehouse auction, then retrofitted with a longer arm to accommodate the blankets.

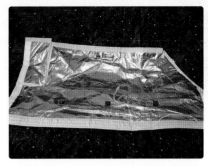

Thermal protection system blanket (back).

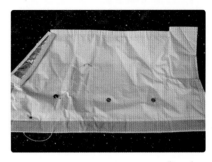

Thermal protection system blanket (front).

Themal protection system blankets (TPSs) line the walls and bulkheads of the shuttles. They were designed to protect astronauts from the dangerous levels of radiation encountered in space. Though made of 20 to 26 layers of silver film and polyester mesh, they are only ⅛ to ¼ inch thick. The silver film was so delicate that TPSs were sewn by hand and installed using ceramic buttons, square-knotted in place.

(photos on this page by Jean Wright)

Jean and her fellow Sew Sisters hand-sewed wheel-well thermal barriers directly to the shuttles. These fabric strips, which sealed the wheel-well doors against the heat of reentry, took four days to make and seventeen hours for two seamstresses to install. (Jean Wright photo)

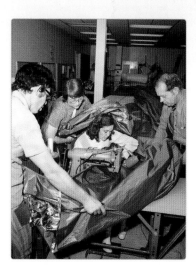

The Sew Sisters sewed with specially engineered threads, including beige quartz thread, which could withstand temperatures of 2,000 degrees Fahrenheit, and bright pink AB 440 thread, which could withstand temperatures of over 3,200 degrees. NASA engineers provided square-headed needles for the seamstresses to use with the thread for hand-sewing. When they discovered that the needles caused the delicate thread to fray, the ladies went to a craft store and bought curved needles to use instead.

(Jean Wright photos)

The exploration of space needed seamstresses even before the space shuttle program. In 1965, NASA selected the International Latex Company to create spacesuits for the Apollo program. The company, also known as Playtex, had previously specialized in making women's undergarments.

An all-female team of seamstresses, including Hazel Fellows (shown here), sewed the spacesuits worn by Neil Armstrong and Buzz Aldrin for their moonwalk during the Apollo 11 mission of 1969. Each astronaut had three custom-made suits: one for training, one for the mission, and one backup. To construct each suit, Hazel and her fellow seamstresses stitched together nearly 4,000 pieces of fabric. (photo courtesy the Smithsonian National Air and Space Museum)

NASA launched its first space station, *Skylab*, into orbit on May 14, 1973. During the launch, the station lost one of its fabric sun shields. The crew, still on the ground, could not safely enter the station until a replacement shield could be installed. Seamstress Alyene Baker (shown here at center) worked with NASA engineers in a race to create a new sun shield before the intense heat damaged the station's interior. Eleven days later, *Skylab*'s crew launched with the replacement shield, which they successfully installed the following day.

(photo courtesy NASA)

During their June 2007 mission to the International Space Station, the crew of the space shuttle *Atlantis* discovered that a corner of one of the thermal blankets protecting the shuttle's Orbital Maneuvering System (OMS) pod had torn loose. Concerned that increased drag during reentry could

cause serious damage or even harm to the astronauts, NASA called on the Sew Sisters to create mock-ups to test repair solutions. At first, NASA engineers suggested sewing the blanket back down, but after testing, recommended that the

Jean Wright at the *Atlantis* exhibit at the Kennedy Space Center. (Ken Kremer photo)

astronauts secure the blanket with surgical staples from the ship's medical kit. During the repair spacewalk, astronaut Danny Olivas stapled the torn corner to an adjoining blanket and inserted additional nickel-chromium pins with the help of a dental probe—also from the ship's medical kit. The staples and pins held the blanket down for a successful reentry. *Atlantis*'s return crew included astronaut Sunita "Suni" Williams, shown at right, who had just broken the female time-in-space endurance record with a total of 195 days in space. (photos courtesy NASA)

Further Reading

NASA Space Shuttle: 40th Anniversary, by Piers Bizony; Motorbooks, 2021.

The Space Shuttle: A Mission-by-Mission Celebration of NASA's Extraordinary Spaceflight Program, by Roland Miller; Artisan, 2022.

Space Shuttle Stories: Firsthand Astronaut Accounts from All 135 Missions, by Tom Jones; Smithsonian Books, 2023.

Sky Walking: An Astronaut's Memoir, by Tom Jones; Smithsonian Books, 2016.

Acknowledgments

Thanks to NASA, the Smithsonian Institution, Jean Wright, and Ken Kremer for the photos in this book's backmatter, and to AirTeam Images and Adrián Valverde for photos I used as illustration references. And a very special acknowledgment to Jean Wright for her generosity in sharing her story and for her tireless help in researching and editing.

Elise Matich is an educator, writer, and artist who lives with her family in an old, quirky house in Alexandria, VA. Her husband and children nourish her creativity through their love, curiosity, and indefatigable imaginations. *Sew Sister* is her first picture book.

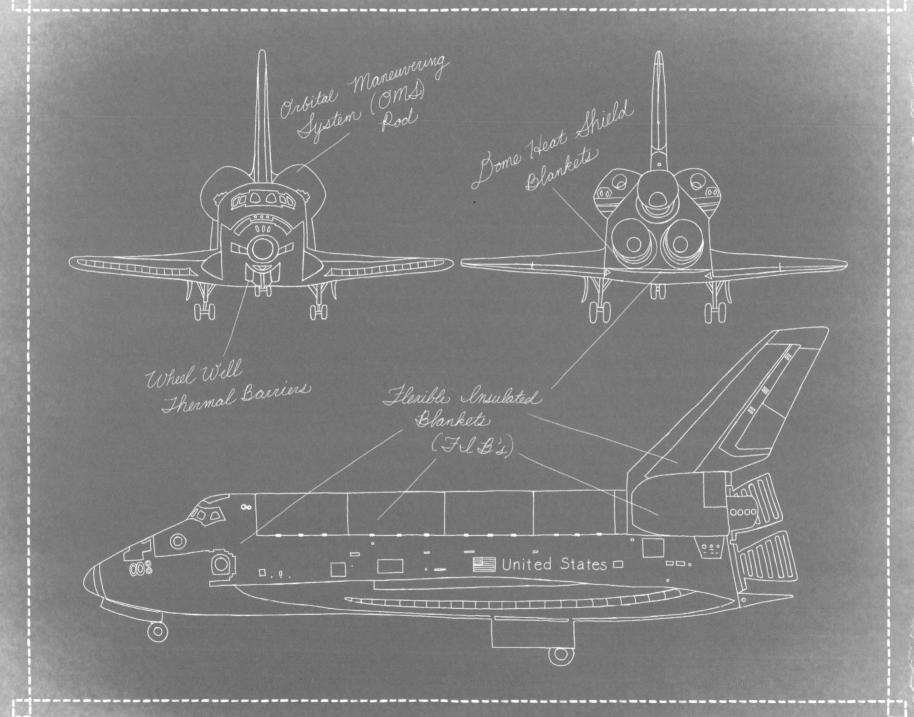

Orbital Maneuvering System (OMS) Pod

Dome Heat Shield Blankets

Wheel Well Thermal Barriers

Flexible Insulated Blankets (FIB's)

United States